Animals in Their Habitats

Pond Animals

Francine Galko

Heinemann Library
Chicago, Illinois

© 2003 Reed Educational & Professional Publishing
Published by Heinemann Library,
an imprint of Reed Educational & Professional Publishing,
Chicago, Illinois
Customer Service 888-454-2279
Visit our website at www.heinemannlibrary.com

Designed by Ginkgo Creative
Printed in China by South China Printing Company

07 06 05 04
10 9 8 7 6 5 4 3 2

Library of Congress Cataloging-in-Publication Data
Galko, Francine.
  Pond animals / Francine Galko.
    p. cm. -- (Animals in their habitats)
Includes bibliographical references (p.   ).
Summary: Explores the animals that make their habitat in ponds.
  ISBN 1-4034-0181-0 (HC), 1-4034-0438-0 (Pbk.)
  1. Pond animals--Juvenile literature. 2. Ponds--Juvenile literature.
[1. Pond animals.] I. Title.
  QL146.3 .G35 2002
  591.763'6--dc21
                        2001007657

Acknowledgments
The author and publishers are grateful to the following for permission to reproduce copyright material:
Cover photograph by Scott Nielsen/NIES/Bruce Coleman Inc.
p. 4 Maresa Pryor/Animals Animals; p. 5 Doug Wechsler/Animals Animals; p. 6 D. Robert Franz/Bruce Coleman Inc.; p. 7 Keith Gunnar/Bruce Coleman Inc.; p. 8 Jim Grace/Photo Researchers, Inc.; p. 9 I. Moar/OSF/Animals Animals; p. 10 Bob and Clara Calhoun/Bruce Coleman Inc.; p. 11 E. R. Degginger/Animals Animals; p. 12 L. West/Bruce Coleman Inc.; p. 13 Harry Rogers/Photo Researchers, Inc.; p. 14 Tom McHugh/Photo Researchers, Inc.; p. 15 Dwight Kuhn/Bruce Coleman Inc.; pp. 16, 22, 23 Zig Leszczynski/Animals Animals; p. 17 Paul Freed/Animals Animals; p. 18 Gilbert S. Grant/Animals Animals; p. 19 Bill Beatty/Animals Animals; p. 20 Nuridsany and Penennou/Photo Researchers, Inc.; p. 21 Hans Reinhard/Bruce Coleman Inc.; p. 24 E. R. Degginger/Bruce Coleman Inc.; p. 25 W. A. Ramaszewski/Visuals Unlimited; p. 26 Brian Kenney/Oxford Scientific Films; p. 27 Scott Nielsen/Bruce Coleman Inc.; p. 28 Jim Balog/Photo Researchers, Inc.; p. 29 Ken Cole/Animals Animals
Every effort has been made to contact copyright holders of any material reproduced in this book. Any omissions will be rectified in subsequent printings if notice is given to the publisher.

Some words are shown in bold, **like this.** You can find out what they mean by looking in the glossary.

To learn more about the mallard ducks on the cover, turn to page 27.

Contents

What Is a Pond?

A pond is a kind of **habitat.** Ponds are small pools of water. The water in a pond stays still most of the time. There is no **current** and there are no waves.

Ponds are **shallow**. A grown-up can touch the bottom of a pond. Plants usually grow in ponds. They grow from the dirt on the pond floor, through the water, and to the air.

Where Are Ponds?

Ponds form in places where water fills
a hole in the ground. Many ponds form
by themselves when rain or melted snow
fills a hole already in the ground.

Other ponds are made by people or animals. Some people dig ponds in their gardens. Beavers often build **dams** on rivers. The dams form ponds.

Pond Homes

Animals make their homes in and around
ponds. You might see a northern water
snake swimming in a pond or warming
itself on a log.

Great pond snails live on the rocks and plants in ponds. They come to the **surface** for air. Their skin can also take in air from the pond water.

Living Along the Edge of a Pond

Many animals live along the edge of the water. Grebes make their nests in the grasses beside a pond. They find food in the pond water.

Yellow warblers live in the willow trees next to ponds. They lay blue eggs in their nests. They catch **insects** near the pond and feed them to their babies.

Living on Top of the Water

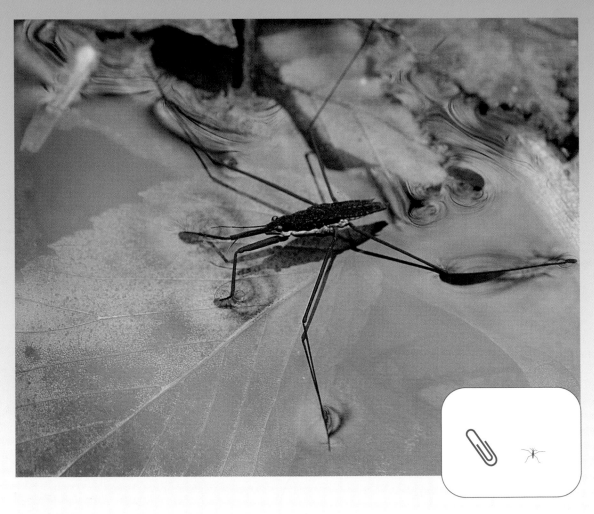

Most pond animals live in or near the water. But water striders live on top of the water! They eat small **insects** on the water's **surface**.

Fisher spiders live under the water and on top of it. They dive underwater to catch small fishes, tadpoles, and insects.

Living in the Water

Many pond animals live in the water. Tench
fishes live in ponds. They eat **insect larvae**
on the pond floor.

Painted turtles like ponds with soft, muddy bottoms and lots of plants. They come out of the water to sun themselves on rocks or logs.

Living on the Pond Floor

Many animals live among the rocks and plant roots on the pond floor. Here, brown catfishes eat other animals and plants in or on top of the mud.

The black-spotted newt is also found on the pond floor. Some newts may leave the water for parts of their lives, but most stay in the water.

Finding Food in a Pond

Ponds have different kinds of food for animals. Jacanas catch **insects** and fishes for food. They also eat the seeds of plants that grow in ponds.

Dragonflies eat mosquitoes and other insects that they catch as they fly. They have strong mouth parts and will even bite if you try to hold them.

Breathing Underwater

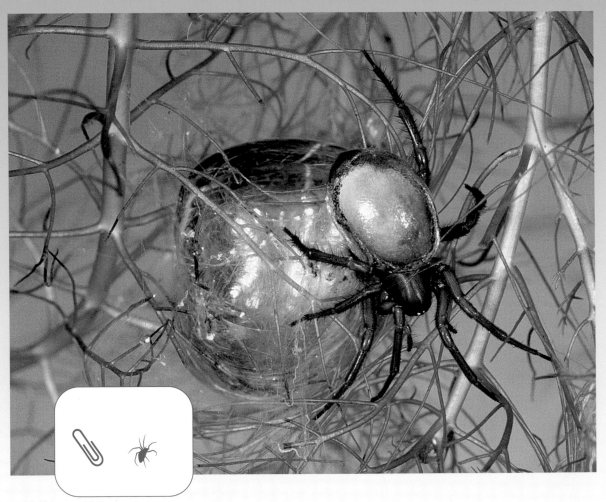

Diving spiders live under the water. They fill their web with air bubbles. The diving spider spends most of its life in its web.

The water scorpion breathes through its long tail! It swims backwards up to the water **surface**. Then it sticks its tail out of the water and takes a breath of air.

Pond Predators

Some pond animals are **predators**. They hunt other animals in the pond. Snapping turtles eat fishes and other pond animals.

Bullfrogs catch and eat small water snakes.
But they have to be careful because large
water snakes catch and eat bullfrogs, too!

Hiding in a Pond

Camouflage is one way to hide from **predators.** Cricket frogs blend in well with the water and plants of a pond.

Often small fishes, or minnows, in a pond are hard to see. Their bodies are the same color as the pond bottom.

Pond Babies

Baby raccoons live with their mothers
near ponds. When they are eight weeks
old, they can leave their **den.** Sometimes
baby raccoons come to ponds to find food.

You may have seen baby mallard ducks swimming with their mother. They eat **insects** in the water and near its **surface**. Baby ducks also hide in the grasses along the edge of the pond.

Protecting Pond Animals

Sometimes rain carries **garden chemicals** into ponds. Some people throw trash into ponds. Chemicals and trash can kill the animals and plants that live in ponds.

You can help keep ponds safe for animals. When you visit a pond, do not throw anything into the water. Always ride your bike on trails near ponds.

 # Glossary

camouflage way an animal hides itself

current movement of water in one direction down a river

dam barrier created when beavers pile sticks on a river bottom until the pile is above the water; a dam usually forms a pond

den animal's underground home

garden chemical thing used to help plants grow, kill weeds, or kill insects that eat plants

habitat place where an animal lives

insect small animal with six legs

larva (more than one are called larvae) very young insect

predator animal that hunts and eats other animals

shallow not deep

surface top of a pond or other body of water

More Books to Read

Giesecke, Ernestine. *Pond Plants.* Chicago: Heinemann
  Library, 1999.

Martin-James, Kathleen. *Building Beavers.* Minneapolis:
  Lerner Publications, 1999.

Taylor, Barbara. *Look Closer: Pond Life.* New York: Dorling
  Kindersley Publishing, 1998.

 Index